D0052236

THE BEST-CASE
SCENARIO
HANDBOOK

by John Tierney

Introduction by Christopher Buckley

WORKMAN PUBLISHING • NEW YORK

Published simultaneously in Canada by
Thomas Allen & Son, Limited.

Cataloging-in-Publication Data is available from the
Library of Congress

ISBN 0-7611-2861-1

Workman books are available at special discounts when purchased
in bulk for premiums and sales promotions as well as for fund-rais-
ing or educational use. Special editions or book excerpts can also
be created to specification. For details, contact the Special Sales
Director at the address below.

Workman Publishing Company, Inc.
708 Broadway
New York, NY 10003-9555
www.workman.com

Design by Barbara Balch

Printed in the U.S.A.

First printing September 2002

10 9 8 7 6 5 4 3 2 1

For Joshua Piven and David Borgenicht
i migliori fabbri

Contents

Introduction

by Christopher Buckley

A few years ago, I got a phone call from *The New York
Times* asking me—in strictest confidence—to write
the citation for its nomination of John Tierney for
a Pulitzer Prize. Never have I more eagerly written
for free. My citation (a thing of beauty) told nothing
but the truth: that John Tierney is not only a brilliant
writer and thinker, but one hell of a lot of fun to
read. He did not get a Pulitzer that year, an injustice
so glaring that I suspect in his heart of hearts he
blamed me for ineptly stating his case.

So when the publisher of this nifty—nay, superb—
little volume asked me to write its introduction, I
was diffident, not wanting once again to impede his
career. In due course, he agreed that if this book
does not become a best-seller, he'll conclude that my
praise is a kiss of death, and a friendship of more
than a quarter of a century will be at peril. So if
you're reading this in the store—please proceed
directly to the cash register. Much is at stake.

But if you require more than a sentimental appeal
to persuade you to buy this book, stop reading the
introduction and open the book to any page. Read

a sentence or two, and you'll be convinced, not only that this book is deliciously, screamingly—or as they say in cyberspace, LOL—funny, but also that one copy will not be enough. Tell the staff you want to buy *all* the copies in the store.

Well, that's *my* best-case scenario, anyway, and probably John's, too.

The inspiration for this book was, of course, the wonderful "Worst-Case Scenario" books by Joshua Piven and David Borgenicht. What's perhaps most amazing about their (richly deserved) success is that at a time when American publishers insist on an often Panglossian upbeat-ness—*You Can Lose 30 Pounds In Eight Hours!*—any book with the word "Worst" in its title should sell so copiously.

But if the "Worst-Case Scenarios" provided the notional nudge, Tierney's "Best-Case Scenarios" is much more than parody. Parody will keep you chuckling for a page or two—beyond that it can become ho-hum, yeah-okay-I-get-it. His book is not just humor, but a practical guide about how to cope with amazing good fortune.

Take, for instance, the chapter on how to respond when your ex-lover publishes a tell-all memoir and names you as "an utter delight in any setting— *especially the bedroom.*" While this has not yet happened to me personally, I remain hopeful, and John's guidance will, I'm sure, come in handy.

I'm also certain that one day, the ATM machine, instead of telling me that I don't have $40 in my account, will accidentally dispense $20,000 in crisp twenties, and deduct it from Martha Stewart's bank account instead of mine. As the saying goes, "It happens." I can, however, personally vouch for the accuracy of the chapter on "How to proceed when you discover which car's alarm keeps going off in the middle of the night." This did happen. It was one of the high points of my life, and John's advice on how to ruin the car owner's life was "Right on!" as we used to say in the Sixties while being tear-gassed.

Well, I could go on, but the Best-Case Scenario in any introduction is that the introducer will state his case and get out of the way. At any rate, I really do have to go, because the lottery just called to tell me that I won $170 million in last night's drawing. *And I didn't even buy a ticket!*

CHAPTER I

Best-Case Moments

How to cope with a broken ATM that will not stop dispensing cash

1. Remain calm.

Do not try to repair the machine. The job can be done safely only by a certified technician.

2. Make sure you're alone.

If others are present, show no surprise as the machine spews thousands of dollars. Explain politely: "I'm afraid I'll be a while. Do you mind going somewhere else? I'd appreciate some privacy." Deflect questions by saying you have "one of the new platinum cards."

If anyone lingers, put on an official air. Pick up the machine's service telephone, if there is one, or lean toward an imaginary microphone on the machine. Speak loudly: "Security. Code 23. Proceed to shutdown mode. Secure perimeter." Tersely order the bystander to exit.

If anyone still lingers, put your face within three inches of his face and snarl, "This is a robbery, you [expletive] moron. You've got three seconds before we blow your fat [expletive] head off." Start counting.

3. Check to see if there are any security cameras.

If not, proceed to Step 4. If there are security cameras, leave the money in front of the machine as though you want no part of it. Pick up the service telephone, if there is one, or pretend to look for an emergency phone number on the machine.

Suddenly throw your hands up in the air. Slowly turn around and gaze in terror at an imaginary armed assailant beyond camera range. Nod obediently. Carry the money to the imaginary assailant.

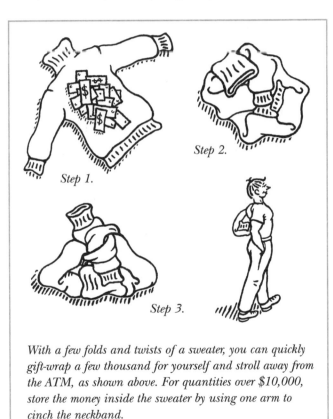

Step 1.

Step 2.

Step 3.

With a few folds and twists of a sweater, you can quickly gift-wrap a few thousand for yourself and stroll away from the ATM, as shown above. For quantities over $10,000, store the money inside the sweater by using one arm to cinch the neckband.

4. Take the money and don't run.

Stuff the bills into your pockets and clothing. Tighten your belt before dumping cash inside your shirt or blouse. For more storage space, tuck your pants into your socks, cyclist-style. To turn a sweater into a valise, seal one sleeve by knotting it at the cuff and use the other sleeve to cinch the sweater just below the neckband. Walk calmly away from the ATM.

5. Stash the cash.

Hide it in a secure place unlikely to be searched by the police. Make no suspiciously large expenditures of cash for at least a year.

6. Tell no one.

Any revelation makes you vulnerable to legal action as well as the expectation by your friends that you'll always be picking up the check.

If you enacted the hold-up drama for the security camera, immediately report your driver's license stolen and get a new one. If bank or police officials later question you, say the assailant took your license and threatened to hunt you down if you reported the crime.

If bank officials continue harassing you, ask them why security was so poor at the ATM facility. Tell them you've been advised to sue. Mention your recurring nightmares.

What to do when a drunken Bill Gates rear-ends your car and mumbles, "Isn't there some way we can work this out without the police?"

1. Demonstrate for him the new digital video camera you just bought.

Replay the footage of him falling out of his car and stumbling up to yours and slurring his words. Point out the "cool" time and date stamp.

Walk Bill back to his car and use the zoom feature to focus in on the labels on the vodka bottle in the dashboard cup holder. Freeze-frame on "80 Proof."

Ask, "Can *you* upload streaming video on your computer?"

Smack your forehead and exclaim, "Can you upload streaming video? You *invented* streaming video!"

2. Ask Bill if he watches *Inside Edition* or *America's Most Embarrassing Home Videos*.

If he doesn't, describe some recent episodes in which titans of American industry were caught on tape in some "really wild situations," including Jack Welch's "hot interview" with that "biz school babe."

3. Go to the nearest ATM.
To locate it, use Bill's wireless Personal Digital Assistant. Insist on driving him. He could hit someone else, and you don't want this to turn into a class-action deal.

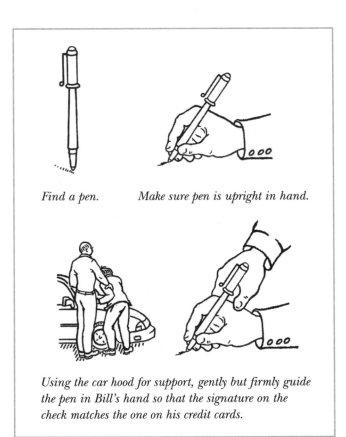

Find a pen.   *Make sure pen is upright in hand.*

Using the car hood for support, gently but firmly guide the pen in Bill's hand so that the signature on the check matches the one on his credit cards.

4. Feed in his bank cards and credit cards until each one is maxed out.

If he's too drunk to remember some of the PINs, find them on his PDA. If the machine runs out of cash—and it may—proceed to another.

5. Help him write a check.

You can fill in the numbers—be sure to count all seven zeros—but he'll have to sober up long enough to sign his name. Thank him, and tell him you'll "hold on" to his PDA until the check clears. ("Just a formality.")

6. Help him home.

Bill isn't known for being a drinker, so he's feeling some unfamiliar sensations. Be sympathetic. Ask what you can do for him, and see that he gets safely to his bed.

7. Deposit the check.

As you wait for the check to clear, amuse yourself by downloading the contents of Bill's PDA into your own computer. You never know when you'll need the personal unlisted phone numbers of America's corporate elite.

8. If you have any problems at all with Windows or any Microsoft program, pick up the phone.

How to respond when, after ten years (and $80,000), your therapist announces, "You're cured."

1. Ask your therapist, "How does that make you feel?"

2. Stop worrying about your overbearing mother, insensitive spouse, ungrateful children, or your secret belief that the Pope is sending messages to you through your right rear molar.

3. Ask your therapist if it's now okay for the two of you to have sex.

If your therapist expresses alarm, say, "Just kidding!"

4. Thank your therapist, but take the opportunity to "clear the air."

Suggested talking points:

- "Eighty grand! What did you *do* with it?"

- "Do you really think it was all my mother's fault? Or were you just saying that to keep me coming back?

- "Remember when I told you about my dream where I was naked at my final exam and I hadn't studied and all my relatives were watching? And Amanda Schwartz was making fun of my hair? How *could* you have fallen asleep?"

- "Enough about me. What's your story, anyway?"

5. After you've handed over the final check, do not ask what your therapist "really" thinks of you. You don't want to know. A candid answer from an unpaid therapist can result in ten more years of therapy.

6. Remind your therapist that the professional code of ethics is still binding with respect to your "embezzlement issues."

How to negotiate with the genie

1. The moment he's out of the lamp, tell him you'll make all three wishes in writing.

Too many people have wasted golden opportunities with offhand comments like "I wish it weren't so darn hot today!" or "I wish I'd brought more sunscreen."

Writing it down gives you a chance not only to think about your wish, but also to avoid tragic misunderstandings. Remember the guy who ended up with a twelve-inch pianist.

2. Ask him what *he'd* like.

Make him feel appreciated, part of your team. How would you feel if you'd been cooped up inside a rusty lamp for the last thousand years, with your captivity only occasionally interrupted by outlandish demands? No wonder genies are so grumpy. *"What am I, anyway, concierge to the world?"*

Maybe he'd just like to hang around outside the lamp for a while, stretching his legs. Let him. A happy genie is a generous genie.

3. Get him telling war stories.

You're not just relationship-building but doing consumer research. This guy wrote the book on wish maximization. He's seen it all. Break the ice by asking him if there really was a drunk who wished for one always full glass of beer and liked it so much he asked for two more. That'll get the genie going.

4. Ask him which wishes historically have made people happiest.

He may tell you that even he can't grant some things (world peace, immortality, noncling plastic wrap). Or he might tell you that in his experience, money really *does* buy happiness. In which case, get him to advise you how to phrase your wish.

You may learn, for instance, that asking for "three billion dollars in a mix of currencies, precious metals, and three-to-five-carat diamonds" is more practical than asking for "all the money in the world." Even if you had room to store it all, do you really want six billion suddenly broke and angry people showing up at your door?

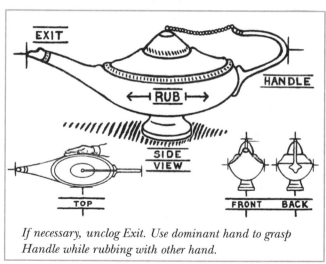

If necessary, unclog Exit. Use dominant hand to grasp Handle while rubbing with other hand.

How to deliver a letter to your boss from his mistress that mistakenly ended up in your in-box

1. Make a copy.
Keep the original in a safe deposit box.

2. Enter his office and close the door behind you.
Hand him the letter and say, "I don't know *how* this ended up on my desk."

3. Ask him how the wife and kids are.
Be sure to use his wife's first name. Explain that you're updating your holiday card list and want to make sure you still have the right home mailing address. Double-check the zip code.

4. As the color drains from his face, look around his office while complimenting him on the expensive furnishings and the sweeping views.
Be especially effusive about his $50,000 Philippe Starck desk. Add that it wouldn't even fit in your "modest rabbit warren."

Pause to give him time to formulate a response.

If he remains stunned and mute, casually quote a sentence or two from the letter: "I'm sitting here

Place mistress's letter on desk within arm's length of family photo. Avoid smirking while asking about wife and kids.

wearing nothing but your diamond choker and a smile. Miss Kitty is getting *soooooo* lonely for Mister Woof-Woof!"

5. When the color returns to his face, ask him, "Woof-Woof? Is he the new guy in Accounting?"

6. Assess his medical condition.

If he remains speechless, he may be waiting for you to talk first. Suggested line: "I've been feeling stalled lately. Where do you see me going in the organization?"

Acceptable responses include:

- "Straight to the top!"
- "All the way!"
- "Sky's the limit!"

Insist on specifics—job title, date, salary, bonus, profit sharing, use of company plane, etc.

7. Suggest that he make a "gesture."

For instance, an immediate "Christmas bonus." If he points out that it's only March, reply, "I like to get my Christmas cards out early."

Add, "Woof-Woof!"

How to accept an Academy Award

1. Do not write your own acceptance speech.
This is not the moment to try out your own material. As soon as you're nominated, call the screenwriter who wrote the part. Thank him effusively. Say: "This nomination really belongs to you."

Ask him to "help," saying that you "want to make sure that everyone involved gets proper credit."

Make him rewrite it twenty-eight times, then fire him and get someone else to "do a polish."

2. Don't typecast yourself.
You may indeed be the first Inuit-Carpathian-American to win Best Actress, but is this really how you want to present yourself to the billion ticket-buyers watching?

Before you call yourself "a vessel" for your "people," ask yourself how many scripts come along with great parts for Inuit-Carpathian-Americans.

However, if you can't resist the tribal urge, speak vaguely about "the incredible support" you've received from "the ICA community." (Non-Inuit-Carpathian-Americans will assume you're referring to your talent agency.)

In deciding which image to leave the audience with—"Leading Lady" or "Earnest Activist"— remember the difference between these roles: approximately $25 million.

3. Have mercy on the viewers.
Keep your speech short. The TV audience has now been watching the world's most self-centered, shallow people congratulate themselves for five and a half hours, interrupted only by commercials. Viewers will bless you for your brevity.

People you absolutely must thank: your agent, "Harvey and Bob," "Steven and everyone at Dreamworks," "and of course [family members you're still speaking to]."

People you really don't need to thank: your stunt double, the "transportation captains" (donut-eating Teamsters), personal trainer, past-life regression therapist. Plus the sap who wrote the movie and the twenty-eight drafts of your acceptance speech.

For maximum sincerity, grasp Oscar with both fists in front of chest (a). For more casual look, use single-fist grip (b) while avoiding common mistakes: lifting Oscar's head above your own (c) or placing thumb too close to Oscar's groin (d).

How to receive a divine visitation

1. Do not look directly into your Visitor's eyes.
Some deities consider this "not done," and a few respond quite badly.

2. Ascertain that it really is God.
Discreetly ask questions that only a deity could answer, but do not be rudely confrontational (e.g., "Okay, Mr. Omniscient, tell me what number I'm thinking of").

Be leery of indirect manifestations. Many bleeding statues and crying Madonnas have been traced to leaky roofs. Before concluding that the sound emanating from the basement is the "Voice in the Whirlwind," check your furnace.

3. Wait patiently for the deity to reveal the purpose of the visit.
Do not ask for money, personal favors, or tricks— mowing your lawn with a sweep of the hand, levitating the toaster oven, and so on. This is God, not a *Bewitched* rerun.

4. Be accommodating but not slavish.
Politely but firmly decline if asked to sacrifice your eldest son.

Celestial motifs are acceptable for packaging shrine water, but any explicit claim of divine endorsement exposes you to legal and other repercussions (lightning, locusts, etc.).

If you are a woman and the deity appears in the form of a swan, close the door and dial 911.

5. Take notes!
You *will* be writing a book. And you don't want it to say, "Then God promised to send a rain of fire and frogs and something else—hubcaps, maybe—over a great sinful city. Either L.A. or Bombay. Or Adelaide. I forget which, but He was really, really mad."

6. Ask for a memento.
Ask God if He or She would mind leaving a little a "souvenir" of the occasion, like a healing spring or roses that bloom in winter.

After the visitation

1. Decide if you want to start a religion.
Make a list of the pros (e.g., large adoring crowds) and cons (large angry crowds).

2. Don't announce the news yourself.
The visitation will be more credible if others reveal it first, like Mrs. McCarthy down the street, whose dog drank out of your birdbath and spoke in tongues.

3. With the advance from your publisher, acquire the surrounding land for future parking and concessions.

CHAPTER II

Best-Case Scenarios at Home

What to do when you catch a burglar in the basement stealing the wedding presents

1. Tell him you have a gun.

If you don't have a gun, stay behind him and repeat threatening comments such as "Don't make me use this."

2. Ask to see his bag.

If it's not big enough, order him to use your extra duffel bags and/or outdated American Touristers. In a pinch, plastic garbage bags will do.

3. Direct him to the closet with the thirty-seven decanters.

Don't pause to speculate why your friends and relatives felt that no marriage is complete without several dozen decanters, including two in the shape of the Empire State Building.

Tell him the old camp trunks would be perfect to hold them all.

4. Point out that he has overlooked the box labeled "Salad Forks and Spoons."

Also the box containing four woks, three ice-cream makers, espresso machine, and moldy humidifier.

To fit more gifts in each box, remove bubble wrap and other padding from all items, especially decanters. Do not be slowed by thief's concern that boxes will shift during transit. When shipping wedding gifts, haste never makes waste.

5. Ask him if he brought a truck.
If he didn't, proceed to Step 8.

If he did, order him to load it with your old exercise equipment, the 1985-era computer, the broken air conditioner, old paint cans, the unusable ladder, Venetian blinds, and the old oil furnace.

6. If he begins to protest that he's not a professional mover, renew your threats to "drill" him "full of holes."

7. Supervise his loading of the truck.
Make sure he pushes large items such as the wok box and the broken rocking chair to the back and stacks things so as to maximize the available cargo space. Orphaned socks and shoes can be crammed into irregular spaces.

8. If he's unable to fit the entire contents of basement into the truck, arrange to FedEx the remaining boxes to him.
Insist on a photo ID with his address for mailing purposes, and demand on-the-spot reimbursement. Figure on two dollars per pound.

9. Report the "theft" to the police.
But not until you've shipped all the remaining boxes!

10. Call your insurance company.
Sound traumatized by your "terrible, irreplaceable loss."

How to cope with a polite teenage child

1. Ask, "What's wrong?"

2. Inspect your car for fresh dents.

3. Look for telltale signs of drug use: persistent smiling, hugging, laughter, insistence on smelling the roses, generalized delight in life.

When your teenager spontaneously embraces you, respond warmly while discreetly patting him down for drugs.

4. If you find no dents or drugs, accept your good fortune.

5. Make sure the teenager is present whenever other parents are invited over.
Act nonchalant when the teenager stands as adults enter the room, shakes their hands while looking them in the eye, and makes effortless small-talk ("Gosh, Mrs. Smith, that's a gorgeous dress!").

When jealous parents express amazement, shrug and say, "We really can't take any credit for it." If they press you for your secret, tell them, "Love. Just love."

6. Innocently ask how their teenagers are doing.
In a chipper tone, inquire: "So, how many nose rings does Sydney have now?"

Listen sympathetically to their tales of woe, interjecting supportive comments:

- "Oh, I wouldn't be too hard on him if I were you. I read somewhere that they all go through a 'swastikas on tombstones' phase."

- "Actually, for most of our evolutionary history, there was nothing at all unusual about a girl being pregnant at age fifteen."

- "They're not really going to prosecute George Junior, are they? It's not as though he actually *lit* the fuse."

How to proceed when you discover which car's alarm keeps going off in the middle of the night

1. Note the license plate.
Once you have the license plate number, you can obtain the name and address of the owner from the Department of Motor Vehicles or from on-line databases. If the owner's phone number is unlisted, knock on his door and explain that the Neighborhood Watch patrol is gathering phone numbers of all residents in order to alert them of any suspicious activity.

2. Disable your phone's outgoing Caller ID.

3. Go to bed early.

4. Set your bedside alarm for 3 a.m.

5. Wake up and call the owner of the car.
Identify yourself as the "Watch Commander" of the neighborhood's new "Auto Alarm Rapid Response Unit."

Report that a "suspicious-looking person" has been observed near the car, and that since its alarm goes off whenever anyone walks by, you were "naturally" concerned and "just had to call and check."

6. Call back at 3:30 a.m.

Apologize if you gave the impression in your last call that his car's security was "not a matter of life and death." Say that all the other neighbors have pledged to "pay any price, bear any burden" to protect his car radio.

7. Call back at 4 a.m.

Say you're "just calling to report" that the neighbors have "established a secure perimeter" around the car. Explain that the "no-walk zone" is "heavily defended" and that he must inform the "Command Center" if he will be approaching the vehicle.

Tell him that when the sentry challenges him with the pass code, "Carnivorous coyotes in Colorado congregate cacophonously," he must reply with an exact imitation of his car alarm. Caution him that the imitation must be "exact" or the situation could "end badly."

Make him practice whoops over the phone.

8. Call back at 4:30 a.m.

Play a tape of the car alarm going off into the receiver. Shout "Code Orange!" Tell him that the "perimeter has been breached" but that the neighbors are "holding the line" while "awaiting reinforcements."

9. Call back at 4:40 a.m.

Say you're calling with "great news"—it was "just a bird" and the car is "secure." Tell him to "rest easy," but emphasize that "this is no time for complacency," as there is still an hour to go before dawn.

10. Call back at dawn.

Tell him that the threat level has been downgraded from Orange to Tangerine.

Assure him that the Command Center will be back on full alert tonight "and every night." Tell him, "The whole neighborhood would be up anyway. Who could sleep, knowing that your CD changer is at risk?"

If car owner's attention wanes after 4 a.m., adjust volume of headset's microphone.

"Shall I starch your T-shirt before dinner, sir? And will you be wearing the Nikes, or something less formal?"

How to get the most out of your butler

1. Hire a Brit.

If cringing servility is a must, then you may want to look elsewhere for your manservant. But at the end of the day, you just can't beat Jeeves. To Americans and other postcolonials, there's nothing so satisfying as the spectacle of a once imperial race reduced to picking your underwear off the bathroom floor.

2. During the interview, ask him to call you by your first name.

If he does, don't hire him.

3. Rely on his discretion—but get it in writing.

He may seem like the most tight-lipped man on the planet, but, frankly, standards have slipped since British butlers began publishing sensational tell-all memoirs about the antics and foibles of their employers. Once the saying went "No man is a hero to his valet." Now, thanks to the valet, he won't be a hero to anyone. Have your lawyer draw up an iron-clad confidentiality agreement.

4. Do not start sounding like him.

It's an "elevator," not a "lift." You have to go to the "bathroom," not the "loo." You wear "suspenders," not "braces."

Go ahead and rhyme "valet" with "mallet," but otherwise stay away from that bloody accent. You'll only sound foolish to your friends and positively mortifying to poor Jeeves.

5. Don't be intimidated.

He may sound better than you, know more than you, be better bred than you, and be more competent than you, but *you* have more money! And in *this* little former British colony, bub, that's all that matters.

If Jeeves forgets his role, buy *Roberts' Guide for Butlers & Other Household Staff*, written in 1827 by an exemplary servant full of tips for brushing hats and polishing mahogany. Leave it on your bedside table opened to "A Word to Heads of Families," in which Mr. Roberts explains: "You, my respected masters and mistresses, will reap the principal advantage of the diffusion of a knowledge of their duties among servants, whose ignorance is sometimes very troublesome." Mr. Roberts proceeds to say that a butler must always defer to your "will and pleasure" because of the cardinal rule of your relationship: "Might is right."

Bottom line: When you want a beer breakfast, Jeeves shows up with a silver tray and a respectful "This Bud's for you, sir."

6. If you get into trouble, remember four words.

The butler did it.

What to do when Santa Claus actually shows up

1. Ask to see some ID.

2. Do not offer him milk and cookies.
He's had quite enough, thank you. The poor man could use a real drink. (Note: Santa knows the difference between "good" Scotch and "bad" Scotch.)

3. Butter him up.
Compliment the cut of his suit (he obviously put some effort into it). Admire his stamina in carrying the bag. "How many chimneys have you lugged that down tonight? Those PlayStations can't be light. Have you been pumping iron?"

4. Once he's comfortable, delicately address the "issues" in your "relationship."
For instance: "Santa, this isn't a criticism, but is there something about me that screams 'bedroom slippers'? Every year?"

5. Suggest he "take a load off."
Sit him down in front of the TV with a *Baywatch* rerun and ask if it would be okay to "just have a peek" in his bag.

Offer him another Scotch.

Switch the bedroom slippers for something you really want—Hermès Birkin bag, box of Cohiba Lanceros, BMW convertible.

6. Help him back up the chimney.

Offer him a boost or, better, a ladder. As he shimmies up the flue, casually shout some constructive hints for next year's presents—jewelry, furs, watches, and so on. "But if it's easier, cash is great, too."

Tell him not to worry about the reindeer residue. But if you need a new roof, now would be an excellent time to point it out.

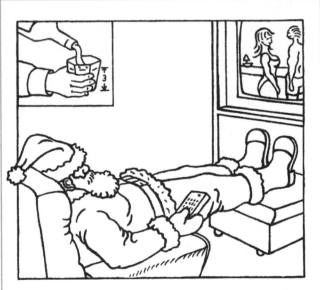

If your television's remote control is not mitten-friendly, lend Santa a hand.

How to contain your emotions when, minutes after 8 o'clock on a Sunday morning, a spark from your neighbor's 175-decibel gas-powered leaf blower sets fire to every tree on his property

1. Immediately park your car in front of the fire hydrant.
This will delay the firefighters just long enough to end the leaf-bearing years of that 200-year-old monster deciduous oak.

2. Celebrate tastefully.
If you own a violin, play it.

3. Offer consolation.
Without smirking, lean over the fence after the fire department has left and say, "Well, Jim, I gotta say, that leaf blower of yours sure did the job! You can say 'Sayonara!' to your leaf problems."

Then ask to borrow it.

4. Go back to bed.

Enjoy the next decade. That's at least how long it should take his replacement trees to produce enough leaves to be worth blowing.

Post-Fire Life Cycle of an Oak

CHAPTER III

Best-Case Food and Drink

What to do in a pretentious restaurant when you're mistaken for the *Times* food critic

1. Remain aloof.
Affect annoyance at being recognized. Gruffly demand to be treated "like an ordinary diner."

2. Don't be limited by the menu.
Hand it back to the maitre d' and say, "I'm just not in the mood for French tonight. Ask Alain to whip me up some risotto with white truffles, and for the main course, pistachio-crusted mahi mahi in a coconut–mango–passion fruit reduction. And for dessert, I just have this *craving* for Heath Bar–M&M soufflé. Is that a problem?"

If the maitre d' says the kitchen doesn't have the ingredients for a dish, shrug and say, "Very well. Then just send a waiter to pick it up from [name of rival restaurant]. They *always* have it."

3. While eating, pretend to dictate into miniature tape recorder.
Sample comments: "Too many notes." "Overeager." "Yuck."

4. If anyone pulls out a cell phone, fly into a rage and demand that it be confiscated.

If yours rings, by all means answer it. Talk as long as you like. When the soufflé arrives, wave it away. Tell the waiter you're phoning in your review. Demand another soufflé.

5. After the first course, announce, "I'll see the kitchen now."

On entering, tell the kitchen staff, "As you were. This is strictly an informal visit." Put on an apron. Ask for some ground beef and a spatula, and demonstrate to the chef how a "real burger" is made. On the way out, stare enigmatically into the chef's saucepan. Exit, shaking your head.

6. When the wine bottle is two-thirds empty, make a face and announce, "It's off."

Suggest they "make amends" by bringing something "with a little more breeding."

7. After the second course, get up and walk outside for a breath of fresh air.

Offer no explanation. The sight of an exiting food critic in mid-meal will inspire terror and confusion. (See Appendix A for a field report by the actual *Times* critic.)

8. Before the check arrives, request the menu again.

Tell the maitre d', "I know my money's no good here, but I'd like to leave you and the chef at least a little something." Autograph the menu and hand it to him.

Offer to pose for a group photograph.

What to do when you're accidentally locked in the cellar at Château Pétrus

1. Do not call for help.
Secure the door to foil rescue attempts.

2. Be selective.
You can't drink it all. Concentrate on 1961, the most celebrated vintage, along with stars from other decades—1929, 1945, 1959, 1970, 1982, 1990. To help remember those years, use the following simple mnemonic device:

$$61 = 29 + 45^{59} - \sqrt{70} + \frac{82\,x}{90}$$

where x is your favorite number in base 2. This will make perfect sense halfway through the first case.

3. Don't glug.
You're not at a Roman orgy. (The Romans never had wine this good.) You're in the world's finest wine cellar—all by yourself.

4. Do not become a slave to a single vintage.
One or two sips per bottle will suffice. Move on!

For fun, blindfold yourself and see if you can tell the difference between the 1945 and the 2000.

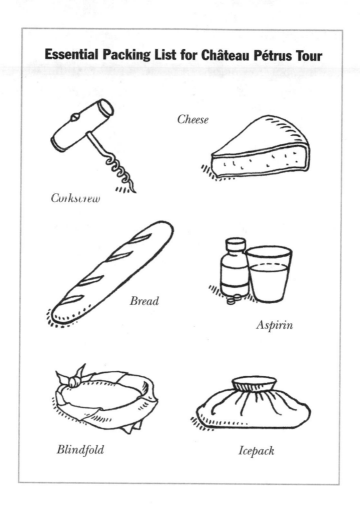

Essential Packing List for Château Pétrus Tour

Corkscrew

Cheese

Bread

Aspirin

Blindfold

Icepack

5. Amuse yourself by pretending that it's a testimonial dinner to yourself.

Give toasts to yourself. Interrupt with "I'll drink to that!" and "Hear, hear!"

6. Experiment.

Many people can claim to have drunk $5,000 bottles of wine, but how many can boast, "I find that the '61 is best when mixed with the '45 with just a splash of the '59. It adds a nice touch of cinnamon to the black currant."

7. Watch out for broken glass.

8. When you're "rescued," take the offensive.

Make no apologies for the eight dozen empties. Tell them you're an alcoholic (probably true at this point) and had been dry for the last twelve years. Refer to the "terrible relapse" caused by their negligence. Say that you'll try to be understanding, but you must first speak with your lawyers.

CHAPTER IV

Best-Case Love and Sex

How to respond when someone you want to dump dumps you first

1. Don't interrupt.
Let them do the talking.

2. Be a martyr.
If they say, "Maybe we should give it another try," shake your head bravely and reply, "No, don't spare my feelings. It'll just be harder for me later."

3. Maximize your martyrdom.
Don't specifically ask to keep the most valuable stuff you acquired together. But speak wistfully about memories associated with various items.

Sample lines:

- "Boy, we sure made some memories on that antique Persian rug, didn't we?"

- "I'll never forget the sun on your hair the afternoon we bought that 52-inch flat screen plasma digital Sony high-definition TV."

4. On the way out the door, say that any further personal contact between you would be "too painful."
Suggest you use as a go-between that friend of theirs you've always had a secret thing for.

Onion-treated eyeglasses lend credibility and confer strategic advantage.

What to do when the geek from your high school class who had a crush on you turns up on the *Forbes* 400 richest list

1. Attend this year's high school reunion.

2. Pretend you haven't seen the list.
Greet him like a long-lost soul mate. Give him the impression you think he teaches math on an Indian reservation in Oklahoma.

Praise his idealism.

Before he can correct you, proceed to Step 3.

3. Rewrite history.
"Confess" that you always "had the hots" for him, but were "too shy" to act on it.

Key line: "I was always afraid I wasn't smart enough for you."

4. Wait for a slow song and ask him to dance.

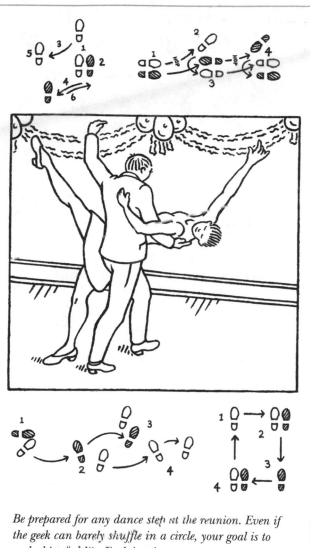

Be prepared for any dance step at the reunion. Even if the geek can barely shuffle in a circle, your goal is to make him feel like Fred Astaire.

What to do when your ex-lover's tell-all memoir depicts you as an "utter delight in any setting— especially the bedroom!"

1. Claim not to have read the book.
Deflect all questions with, "I'm happy for all her recent successes."

2. Promote the book relentlessly.
Buy up large quantities of the book at stores monitored by the bestseller lists.

Hire a publicist to plant items in gossip columns suggesting that George Clooney, Josh Hartnett, and other hunky celebrities she slept with are "furious" at you for "showing them up."

3. When the movie comes out, with Brad Pitt playing you, sue.
Issue a statement: "As an intensely private person who values emotional commitment, I am deeply embarrassed by the film's portrayal of me as a rakish Adonis with extraordinary sexual powers."

When questioned, concede that you can't point to any specific factual errors.

How to proceed when, shortly after the expiration of your pre-nup with a $900-million corporate mogul, you discover that he gave more than just an interview to the editor of the *Harvard Business Review*

1. Call the editor.

Ask how the interview went. Ask if it's running with photos of your husband in knee socks.

2. Call the journal's other editors and board of directors.

Profess ignorance about journalistic ethics. Ask, "Do *all* editors of the *Harvard Business Review* sleep with folks they're interviewing?"

3. Curl up in a comfy chair with a legal pad, calculator, and a copy of your state's community property law.

Using a yellow marker, highlight the section about dividing marital assets fifty-fifty.

Interview with the Harvard Business Review: $450 million.
Divorce from a philandering cad: Priceless.

With a calculator manufactured by your husband's company, divide $900 million by two.

Smile.

Repeat.

Smile again.

4. Hire a lawyer.

5. Call your husband.
Ask if the interview was worth $450 million.

How to respond when your girlfriend or wife says, "Honey, for your birthday, would you like to try a threesome?"

1. Resist the temptation to say, "Is the Pope Catholic?"

This could be a trap. Make sure that her definition of "threesome" does not include Vittorio the tennis pro. This is *your* birthday.

2. Do not suggest any names!

This could be a ploy to find out which of her friends you lust for. In that case, you'll never hear the end of it. So many men have fallen for this con that marriage counselors have a name for it: The Bermuda Triangle.

Casually ask, "Oh, I don't know, honey, who'd *you* have in mind?"

3. If she says, "Well, there's that personal trainer at the club, you know, the one who used to model for Victoria's Secret? She's always talking about how cute you are, and she's mentioned at least a

dozen times how she loves threesomes. She wasn't exactly subtle. I could always ask her," reply, "Okay."

4. Remain calm.

Shrug and say, "It *is* my birthday. I was looking forward to those golf clubs. But I suppose this is something we could share."

How to cope when you discover that your husband isn't spending his weekends hunting deer—he's actually hunting antiques

1. Make sure he isn't gay.

2. Tell him not to be ashamed.
Mention that you just read "somewhere" that Arnold Schwarzenegger also "lives to antique" and "goes wild" at collectibles auctions.

3. Throw out the guns, camouflage gear, orange-blaze hats, elk antlers, moose heads, and elephant-foot bar stools in his Potemkin "den."

4. Purchase the current edition of *America's Quaintest Bed and Breakfasts*.

5. Trade in his Humvee for a Volvo station wagon.

6. Spend weekends together blissfully bidding on colonial weather vanes.

The Thrill of the Hunt

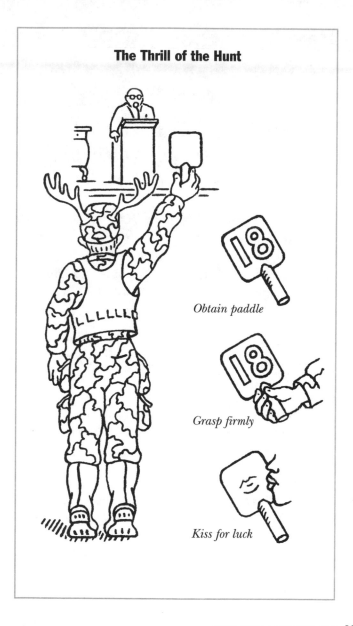

Obtain paddle

Grasp firmly

Kiss for luck

How to respond when your lover says, "Darling, if we're going to spend $25,000 on a dress, don't you need *just* the right necklace to go with it?"

1. Appear pensive.

Stare into the mirror at the dress and say, "It does seem to need *something*. I wouldn't have thought a necklace—but you have a much better eye for this sort of thing than I do."

2. Pause.

Keep staring into mirror as if genuinely conflicted.

3. Graciously compromise.

Suggest consulting an "impartial" authority: "Let's call [name of your favorite jeweler] and see what he thinks."

4. Move quickly.

Immediately use your cell phone to phone the jeweler. Keep a straight face while explaining your "predicament." Suggest that the jeweler needs to see the dress with you in it—right away. If you're calling from a yacht, tell him your precise latitude and longitude.

A Pocket Guide to Diamonds

Hexabril

Dogwedge

Marcian

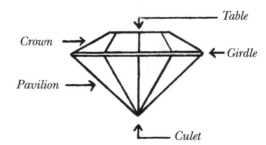

5. Let the jeweler do the rest.

When he arrives with half of South Africa's diamond output along with Catherine the Great's favorite ruby and pearl pendant, let the jeweler demonstrate why your lover needs to spend the GDP of Rhode Island in order to preserve his self-respect.

6. Flaunt the necklace strategically.

At social occasions, when jaws drop and eyes widen, feign embarrassment and mild annoyance. Complain about the security concerns. "Lloyd's tried to make me ride here in a Brinks truck, but I put my foot down. You can't let this run your life."

Emphasize that you'd never have bought it for yourself. "It's not really me. But it means so much to him."

How to get the biggest bang for your buck when you discover that your couples therapist accepts bribes

1. At the end of a session, as your wife turns to leave, reach out to shake your therapist's hand.
Slip two crisp, folded $100 bills into his palm. Say, "I hope we can make some *real* progress next week." Wink and follow your wife out the door.

2. After your wife is asleep, fax your therapist some suggested "talking points" for next week's session.

3. At the next session, remain expressionless when the therapist says, "At the end of the day, any couple needs a bond. You need to be on the same team."

4. Follow the script.
You (earnestly): "You're absolutely right.
    Maybe I could join her book club."

Therapist: "I'm talking about real *quality* time.
    Just the two of you."

You: "Okay. I'm game. I shouldn't be spending
    all my time alone in the garage."

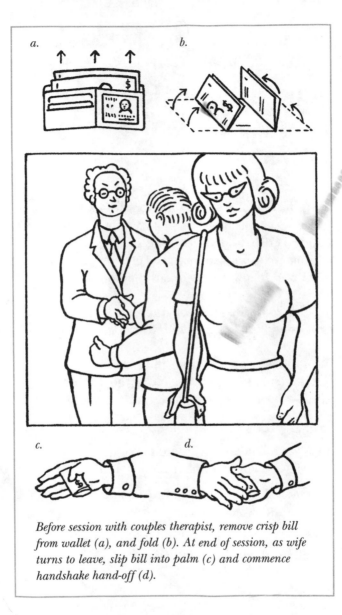

Before session with couples therapist, remove crisp bill from wallet (a), and fold (b). At end of session, as wife turns to leave, slip bill into palm (c) and commence handshake hand-off (d).

Wife: "If you spent as much time with me as you did with that Corvette—"

Therapist: "Exactly! You need to spend that time together. *Both* of you. You *both* need to work on 'that Corvette' together."

Wife (paling): "What?"

Therapist: "Sure. Go home right now. Make a new start. Change out of that Prada pantsuit into your tightest blue jean cutoffs and get down under that hood. Replace the fan belts, check the plugs, grease the bearings. Pop open a couple of frosties. Put the game on! You'll be rebuilding more than a car. You'll be rebuilding your marriage."

Wife: "You must be—"

Therapist: "Well, I see our time is up for today."

5. After your wife has stormed out, slip your therapist another $100.

6. On the ride home, give your wife time to "process."
Once at home, break the icy silence with, "Honey, this marriage means everything to me. I'm willing to put the work in. Are you?"

7. Surprise your wife on her birthday with the latest Pirelli calendar and a new set of monogrammed spanner wrenches.

How to respond when your lover reveals that he or she has the same favorite twisted, disgusting, perverted, unspeakable, revolting sexual fantasy as you

1. Do not say, "Eee-yooouu, gross!"

2. Make a shopping list: uniforms, fruit, collars, Reddi-wip, restraints, feathers, rubber tubing, and so on.
Don't forget extra batteries.

3. Go shopping.

4. Turn off the phone.
Leave a message on your answering machine saying that you'll be out of town on business for "the foreseeable future." Be sure to add that the machine won't be accepting messages, and even if it did, you certainly won't be monitoring them.

5. Climb every mountain.
Yodel "Yes! Yess! Yessss!"

CHAPTER V

Best-Case Travel

How to fly first class

1. Purchase a discounted coach ticket.
To improve your odds, pick a flight that has at least four seats open in first class.

2. Look rich.
Shorts, tank tops, and jogging outfits do not impress airline check-in personnel. Encase your body and your possessions in thin, expensive materials. Carry only the newest and smallest travel toys. Use luggage tags that keep your name covered—no true V.I.P. wants to be revealed to the masses.

Bring very little aboard. A mogul leaves the schlepping to assistants, and a sophisticated traveler realizes that the odds of losing a checked bag are miniscule now that airlines are matching luggage with passengers before each flight.

3. Slip a crisp bill into your ticket folder.
Figure on $50 domestic, $100 international.

4. At the airport, proceed to the first-class check-in.
Give the impression you want to buy a full-fare first-class ticket. Ask: "Any room up front on [number of flight] to [city or, for larger airports, three-letter code] today?" (This is how airline personnel and travel pros put it among themselves.)

If the answer is yes, smile knowingly and hand the ticket folder containing the bribe to the agent. Say, "Any possibility of an upgrade?"

If the answer is no, discreetly remove the money from the folder and hand over the ticket. At least you've finessed checking in at first class. Pause to contemplate the half-mile-long check-in line for economy class.

At the gate, ask again if there is any room "up front" in the event of no-shows. If answer is yes, reinsert the bribe in the ticket folder and repeat the step above.

Don't waste your time in the gate area ingratiating yourself with the flight attendants, who have no authority to order upgrades. Concentrate on the senior gate agent. Also look for an employee behind the counter who's not in uniform and has a two-way radio and a lot of keys. This is the "special services" representative for the flight, who has the authority to order *anything*.

Praise airline personnel: "Considering the pressure you're under at this terminal, the quality of service is just remarkable. I know the company's got problems in other places—I hear about them every weekend from [first name of airline's president]. But he'll be glad when I tell him the story around here."

Be seen noting names of employees. They know they'll be rewarded for a commendation from a frequent flyer. They also know it looks bad if they leave paying customers in coach while giving away empty seats up front to off-duty airline employees along for a free ride. This form of professional courtesy is so common on some airlines that the first-class cabin is referred to as the "employee lounge." Make them share it with you.

5. Once you've got the upgrade, hang back.
When they announce boarding "for our first-class passengers," do not be among the first to leap.

Security personnel charged with doing the "random searches" delight in class warfare against pampered spendthrifts. Wait until they're busy emptying the Fendi purses and Armani pockets of eager-to-board first-class passengers before presenting your ticket.

6. On board, act as if you paid full first-class fare.
For all they know, this seat cost you five grand. For the next seven hours, *they* work for *you.*

Don't delightedly open the overnight kit or play with the seat, foot rest, or various buttons. As you settle into your Barcalounger-sized seat, complain languidly to your seatmate: "First class certainly isn't what it used to be."

Find fault with the hot towel ("practically room temperature") and the Dom Pérignon ("clearly *not* the '93").

To the Manner Borne

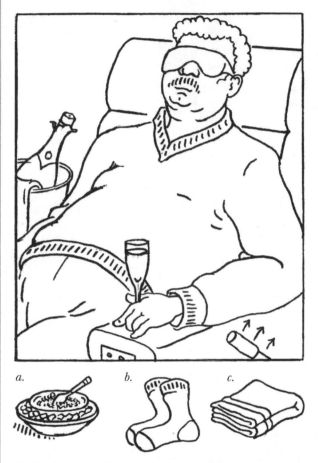

Caviar (a), complimentary socks (b), and hot towels (c) are just some of the amenities first-class travelers should expect.

If you're attracted to the flight attendant, don't be shy. Brush-offs are automatic in the rest of the plane, but not here. Meeting the rich and powerful is one of the main reasons that attendants vie to work up front.

7. Defend your turf!
If anyone from business class tries to use the lavatory, make a scene.

8. But be magnanimous in victory.
After lunch, take a stroll into business class, bringing with you any leftover food (caviar, lobster tails, gravlax, etc.). Offer it to the person you had evicted from the first-class lavatory, saying, "No hard feelings, I hope."

If the person icily declines, saying he has had lunch, express surprise—"Oh, they serve food back *here*?"— while looking about the cabin as if it were a damp cave.